The Journey

I0117909

Paula Cable

chipmunkapublishing
the mental health publisher

Published by
Chipmunkapublishing
PO Box 6872
Brentwood
Essex CM13 1ZT
United Kingdom

http://www.chipmunkapublishing.com

Chipmunkapublishing gratefully acknowledge the support of Arts Council England.

Author Biography

I was born in 1967 in Cambridge, where I grew up with my two brothers and parents.

After graduating from the University of Newcastle with a degree in psychology, I moved to Leeds to study a PGCE in teaching; here I met my husband.

We soon started a family and it was at this point that I began my relationship with mental health as I suffered severely with post natal depression. Following the birth of my second son I suffered yet again, this time I spent a period of time in hospital and underwent Electro Convulsive Therapy. Since then I have had great empathy for those who suffer with mental health issues. It is due to my previous experiences that I have felt so compassionate towards my son when he too suffered with mental health problems; that as well as a very strong maternal bond. Writing this book has been so therapeutic for all involved.

Really this book is a family effort and as such there are 4 authors! We are a happy strong family unit who love to enjoy life and all that it involves...we hope you like our book!

Paula Cable

Dedication

We would like to dedicate this book to all those who have helped us along our journey; especially to the fabulous team of staff in student support at Benton Park School. Thank you!

Paula Cable

Our Big Journey! By Mum

Where to begin?

Where to begin is the question I ask myself as I sit here, lap top in front of me, mind busy whirling! I guess the reason for writing this would be a good start...

Over the last 5 months my family and I have been exposed to an intense roller coaster of emotions as our eldest son, Dan, has begun his transitional journey to secondary school. To say that the transition process has not been a smooth one is the understatement of the century! It wouldn't be fair to blame all the anxiety experienced by Dan on the transition process itself: he showed signs of anxiety and stress towards the end of his primary school life after being diagnosed with a multiple tic disorder just a couple of weeks before leaving primary school. Prior to his diagnosis he suffered for many months from all sorts of body tics and twitches including: neck and head movements, face contortions, leg and arm jerks as well as the odd vocal tic. The frustrations that Dan experienced as he slowly lost control of his body, as the tics took over, were intense and painful to see. He had so much to contend with as he worried about being different from his friends; as he experienced continuous pain from the constant movements; as he was constantly exhausted from trying, desperately, to keep the tics under control. This was really where all his upset and anxiety began; the transition process just further compounded his worries!

Not only did Dan have these two major factors in his life to contend with, he also had the added worry of the medication that was prescribed to help get his tics under control. Dan was given the drug Haloperidol to help reduce his symptoms. Unfortunately, he was told, at the youthful age of ten, that the medication carried its own concerns and serious side effects: in summary, it could be **life threatening** in its own right. This news Dan (his Dad and I) found hard to come to terms with; it certainly added to the levels of stress and anxiety he was experiencing.

We do acknowledge that Dan was always going to find the transition process a challenge, he would always have had his concerns, but never in our wildest dreams did we anticipate the problems that came after that first day at 'Big School'.

By sharing with others our family experience of the transition process, we hope to help others who are facing similar problems. It has become clear that Dan is not alone in his reaction to starting secondary school: others have experienced similar problems. Often the children who find the transition process hard have other challenges going on in their lives at the same time: health issues or other personal problems. One thing that we do know would have helped us over the last few months is reading about other peoples' journeys - maybe we would not have felt so alone and, at times, desperate. Having spoken to Dan at the time of writing this I know that he shares a desire to help others as well, as such he is keen to write his part of the story. We have included some of the many solutions we found along our way, solutions that have moved us just that little step further to the place we all wanted to be: settled and happy. Obviously these solutions have worked for us and if someone else can benefit in any way from reading about them then surely something good has come from our experience.

Hence the reason for putting pen to paper, or should I say fingers to key board? You never know, it just might be a little bit therapeutic too.

The summer before Secondary School

Dan had been looking forward to starting secondary school over the summer holidays. Luckily we had just had a fabulous holiday in Spain, laughing, swimming and eating the 2 weeks away, (what else are holidays for?). We came back to England with 2 weeks left before the start of term and we busied ourselves seeing friends and family; making the most of the time left before life became hectic again.

As Friday, the beginning of term approached, the usual first day nerves were beginning to emerge but nothing more than you would expect. Typical questions were being asked such as: Who do you think will be in my form? What if I get lost? What if I get a red mark? Do you think I will have loads of homework? Despite these questions, despite the hard time we had experienced at the end of year 6, on the whole, everything was happy in our household.

The Big Day Arrives

Dan got up on his first day with a mixture of nerves and excitement. He had arranged to meet up with three friends which he was very happy about. With breakfast inside him and his bag on his back, his brother and I waved him off; I wasn't sure who was more nervous, him, his Dad or me!

It was a long day as I imagined Dan in every lesson, buying his lunch, on the playground and talking to his friends. I also imagined him standing there on his own with no one to talk to - surely every Mother does this? The first day had been planned well by the school as only the year 7s were in so that they could get their bearings before the mad bustle with the other years started.

Eventually the day came to an end and a very happy, confident Dan appeared home. He walked up the road: friend in tow; tie half undone; hair a scruffy mess; bag slung over his shoulder and a big smile on his face. He recalled the day in immense detail and seemed to be quite happy with his lot. And then it started...

As bedtime approached Dan became quite tearful.

Suddenly he was worried about the Monday ahead as he realised just how different secondary school was. The worry of getting lost; being with all the other children; meeting so many new teachers; receiving red marks and **god forbid,** a detention, it all became too much. Instead of remaining in his confident mood the tears began to flow. He began to change in front of our very eyes. To say that Dan was anxious didn't seem to do it justice; instead it felt as if he was being taken over: consumed by terror. The only way we could calm him down, even attempt to get him to sleep, was to say that we would take him down to the school the next day (Saturday) and try to use the map he'd been given to help orientate him. This we did; the caretaker even helped us to look around! This seemed to help considerably and Dan managed to pull himself together and we all breathed a sigh of relief.

Our weekend passed by with regular references to the daunting week ahead but we hoped that these worries were nothing more than the usual year 7 concerns.

The First Full Week

Monday morning came and so did the tears! Dan was really worried now and getting him to leave the house was a massive feat. His anxiety had worked itself up so much that he was actually being physically sick and crying, he had no appetite for breakfast, but still he went out of the door as the rest of us set off for work and school as well. We

all felt upset and anxious.

The week progressed in a similar way with regular tears and episodes of being sick as well as lots of anxious talk and a very low mood in the house in general. During the school day Dan was also texting me, saying how I needed to come and get him, to help him, that he could not cope (the texts were hard to read to say the least and tested my strength completely). Over the course of the week, Dan had also become very obsessed with his health. He was worried about every headache; every tummy ache - he seemed convinced that he was very ill - this was something new for Dan, something we hadn't seen before. Still, we hobbled along to Friday and were hopeful for a good weekend - thank goodness, the week was over! Little did we know that what lay in store for us was even worse.

The Worst Four and a Half Weeks Ever!

Things went from bad to worse over the next four and half weeks. Dan was now being sick 3 or 4 times a day, if he wasn't actually sick he was constantly reaching and was very distressed. He was hardly eating, always crying and clinging on to me - literally! The only way he could be encouraged to get out of bed in the morning was for me to dress him item by item as he cried and begged for me to believe that he was truly ill and unfit for school. Rapidly he seemed to lose all ability to think rationally; he was consumed by fear -

fear of being ill with no one actually taking him seriously. It was also becoming clearer that Dan had a real obsession with me: he could not bear to be apart from me. Dan had begun to follow me around the house like a little dog. If I was in the kitchen so was Dan, if I was having a bath Dan was sitting by the side of the bath talking to me. He had reached the point where he would constantly time me with his watch as I carried out a task; desperate for me to have my hands free so that I could hold and hug him - reassure him that all would be ok. I think the best way to sum up what was happening was that Dan's behaviour seemed to be regressing to that of a toddler. This was so hard to live with, I found it suffocating; I couldn't even go to the toilet without being questioned.

Through all of this I felt physically sick, desperately sad. I had begun to find it hard to sleep, spending half my night worrying about the morning battle ahead. My head was constantly churning over ideas, trying to get to the bottom of Dan's problems. I was lost and felt totally useless; I was truly stressed about the whole situation.

At this point I should also make it clear that before any of this had happened Dan had been a very confident, independent 10 year old. I could leave him in the house happily for a couple of hours on his own, trust him to go to the local supermarket and certainly be away from him for a whole day with no concern on his part.

It was Dan's obsession with me that made me

question how he would ever settle in at school; how could he survive the seven hours at school if he couldn't even bear me to be out of the room for two minutes? He had resorted to wanting to sleep in the same bed as me, (which I have to say I let him), in a desperate attempt to seek some comfort in the mess that was. Dan's obsession with me and his frantic concern for his own health made me question further what it was that was upsetting him so much: it simply could not be the transition to Secondary School alone?

Thankfully, Dan was sleeping well, partly due to the medication that he had been put on for his tics, partly because he was exhausting himself from all the tears and physical symptoms that the stress was causing. In the first few weeks I visited the doctors so regularly as everyone, including us, felt sure that something physical must be wrong. I seriously thought that he must be depressed. It was his ability to sleep that the doctors hung on to – apparently he could not be depressed if his sleeping patterns were still ok!

Whilst things at home were very fraught, at school they were just as bad. Dan was now spending time in the Student Support Centre (a centre set up in the school to help children who required extra support for whatever reason) for a large part of the day instead of taking himself to lessons. On many occasions the school would phone me as Dan had gone to a member of staff saying how unwell he was feeling, how he needed to come home. He was crafty; he would always find someone new that didn't know the situation. I used to imagine that Dan saw the school as a prison, that he would spend all his time planning ways to escape and that it was my job to make sure that all the exits were firmly blocked. It took some time, and a few occasions of me actually having to leave work to go and collect him, for us to all realise just how desperate he was to come home, how he would try anything to get there. I remember clearly arriving on one occasion to pick Dan up from the reception only to dissolve into tears on arrival. The receptionist called for the school nurse to come and talk to me, to calm me down before they brought Dan out; it was all so very difficult.

By making sure that all school staff were aware of the situation with Dan he began to realise that it wasn't that easy to get sent home. If he felt ill he would be sent to The Student Support Centre who would then take charge. This process made it harder for Dan to be sent home and so again I felt that we were back in control. However, to complicate things further Dan started lying about how he felt, making up symptoms, exaggerating problems. This created problems for the staff in the support centre and for us because of his tic medication, Haloperidol. On starting this medicine we had been given a list of symptoms to watch out for, a list of possible side effects of the medication that could be serious. Trying to work out whether Dan's ailments were real, medication induced, stress induced or indeed altogether imaginary was a skill the school and I were developing fast. We were always mindful of the fact that Dan's symptoms could be those that we had been told to look out for; they could be connected to the tablets. This all just served to make things much more complicated than they needed to be. One thing I held in my mind at all times that helped me keep my patience with Dan was that these symptoms were very real to him - he truly believed he was very ill.

So what was wrong?

Whilst this had all been going on we had been desperately trying to work out what the real problem was. We knew it wasn't simple and piecing together all parts of the puzzle I finally began to understand what the problem could be. Having been told that he was taking tablets that he thought could be life threatening and having been given a list of symptoms to watch out for; Dan had put two and two together and had come up with five. All the symptoms that he had been asked to look out for were similar to the symptoms you would expect if you were suffering from anxiety. Dan was suffering from these anxiety symptoms due to being in a new school, he had therefore come to the wrong conclusion and thought that he was experiencing the side effects listed for his medication and that he could die. His obsession with me was easily explained as well - if he thought he was going to die because of his tablets then he simply needed his mum to be with him - no one else would do! I challenged Dan with my theory and with HUGE tears rolling down his cheeks he cried **'At last someone understands me!'** He was so relieved that at last someone had put his fears into words, someone had understood his distress, that he just sat crying and hugging me for ages. I cried too! This was all well and good but now we needed some serious help in order to begin the process of changing Dan's beliefs. Just simply telling him that his tablets were fine wasn't enough, he didn't believe it. He believed that, as sure as night followed day, his tablets could kill him! He had got the whole thing so out of perspective it was going to be a mammoth task to sort it all out.

The obvious answer to every one was to tell him to stop taking the tablets; so many people suggested this I actually began to feel quite bad that I didn't make him do just that. However, even suggesting that he should stop the tablets created problems: he was so scared of the tics returning and being back to square one, being in pain and feeling so different!

In the early days I had tried getting cross with him when he got himself in to one of his incredible states, but that made matters worse. In the end our mantra was be firm and fair.

My Life on Hold

Work for me was becoming harder and harder as I was constantly being interrupted during the day (as a teacher this was even more of a problem than had I been working in an office!). Dan would ring and text regularly, the support staff, at my request, would also ring and ask questions. They wanted me to know just how bad he was, whether I was happy with the symptoms that he was showing i.e. should we concern ourselves with the tablets?

Getting out of the house in the morning was becoming almost impossible which was making me late not to mention the upset all this was having on our younger son. With all the focus on Dan, our youngest son (Tom) felt left on the sidelines. After five weeks of Dan's constant crying, worrying, being sick, poor old Tom was beginning to get tearful and upset too. I now found myself having to go into his school regularly as well, explaining why he too was so upset and tearful; something was going to have to change. I was starting to question my own ability to cope with the stress involved. Certainly, work was beginning to suffer which was not fair on the children in my class or on my fantastic job share partner. (An absolute rock!). I found myself feeling low as well, I was beginning to wake up in the night worrying, my stomach was constantly churning and I too, was regularly feeling sick!

One morning, when things were worse than usual the decision to make a drastic change to what was going on was taken out of my hands. After an awful evening with Dan crying from the moment he'd arrived home up until bed time followed by a restless night's sleep for me, Dan was yet again refusing to go to school, I'd cleared up three piles of sick, Tom was crying and my husband was struggling to know what to do, he was in tears too! It was literally impossible for me to leave the house for work as Dan clung on to me screaming and crying. I had tried to talk to all the family, to get them to rally around but to no avail. I had no choice: I picked up the phone, made my apologies and excused myself from work. The time had come to put my family first and concentrate on the job in hand before things got even worse. We certainly couldn't carry on the way we were, something had to change.

That Tuesday was the turning point for us all for many reasons.

Extra Help at Last!

Throughout these past five weeks we had been flying solo. When I say solo I mean that the staff from the Student Support Centre at school and I had been managing the situation as best we could, but it was a case of crisis management! The Student Support Centre had become our lifeline. To say that the staff there were amazing really does not do justice, they were **incredible.** Some mornings I had to resort to driving a screaming and crying Dan to school, clinging on to me for dear life, throwing up on the way. The staff at the support centre would greet us with that knowing look, try to settle Dan, while I walked away leaving them to it - tears in my eyes. He would spend most of the day in the centre with them as they tried to reason with him, trying to encourage him to return to classes etc. Some days they were successful, he would manage a couple of lessons, and other days he would just sit and cry, often throwing up and saying how ill he actually felt. On one occasion, he got so distressed that he passed out and it was questioned whether he had actually had a mini fit! Some days he would test their strength, he was so sure he was ill that it took nerves of steel to believe that anxiety could possibly be the cause of Dan's symptoms. They never seemed to tire of us, never lose their patience; I couldn't believe what an oasis we had found.

It did cross my mind on several occasions that school might just say that they could longer cope with Dan, then where would we be? There are not many people you can trust with your poorly child who is so distressed that he displays so many physical symptoms, but trust them I did and still do – COMPLETELY!

I had taken Dan to the doctors so many times during these first few weeks at secondary school, begging for help. They put him on the waiting list to see the Child and Adolescent Mental Health Service (CAMHS), but the wait was so long. One particular evening when things had got so bad at home, Dan ended up saying he would rather not be alive, he wanted to be dead! He paced his room for over half an hour talking to himself, muttering all kinds of things, all of which were so hard and painful to hear. It was at this point that I became more determined than ever that someone had to listen to us, how could I just sit back and watch my son crumble away? The next day I rang the doctor demanding an emergency meeting with the CAMHS team. I ended up speaking to a wonderful receptionist who listened to my tears. She had a nephew in a similar situation and assured me that she would help and help she did! Our appointment came through for the following day- professional help at last!

Dan was quickly assessed over the period of a couple of appointments and it was decided that he should receive some cognitive behaviour therapy, but, guess what? There was a six month waiting list! This seemed to be the story of our lives. For every time our hopes were raised something else would come along and crush them. How could we go on like this for the next six months without concrete advice and treatment? I like to think of myself as a very polite and understanding person; I had learnt however over the last few weeks that sometimes you have to speak your mind - so I did! It wasn't easy to plead our case as I found it hard to get the words out due to my tears; however, the CAMHS lady listened **and heard** me. I later found out that she had put Dan to the top of the waiting list so what was to be a six month wait, turned into a six week one! Now that I knew what treatment Dan was awaiting I decided to get reading. I went straight to the internet and ordered some books on cognitive behavioural therapy for children. I was after all a teacher used to children, a mother determined to help her son and a very good reader; surely I could start to understand the situation better? This was a good decision as it gave me some direction, a purpose. It made me feel so much better: useful and in control again.

At the same time as this I had been pursuing other avenues of help including chasing up the educational psychologist. Again after a lot of phone calling and begging, an appointment for the educational psychologist finally materialised. This appointment was a godsend as Dan and I sat and explained exactly what was going on. Their immediate response was to say that due to everything that had happened to Dan: the tics, the medication, the transition process, the result was that Dan was suffering from extreme separation anxiety from me. They acknowledged straight away that we could not go on as we were, something had to change.   This was indeed music to my ears as this appointment had ended up being on the same day that I had been signed off work for 5 weeks. This meant that I was in a position to get more involved in Dan's day, which I'd felt for some time was necessary, if we were to make any progress at all. At this meeting there was also talk about Dan not being able to manage mainstream school: maybe he needed to spend some time at Special School, a school for children with emotional needs. While I knew things had to drastically change I became determined to avoid this at all costs; I knew Dan could settle given time and lots of support and I also knew that the last thing he needed was yet more changes. An alternative suggestion was that Dan was introduced more slowly into secondary school by going in for just a lesson at a time and then building this up. Having observed him over the course of the first five weeks I had seen that Dan could normally manage the last lesson of the day. He was able to reason with himself that after this lesson he could see me. Using this fact I thought that he could cope with more than just going to school for one lesson at a time. I thought that if I could go in and see him, split his day up, then he would probably be able to begin to settle in. This surely would be a quicker and less disruptive method of helping him.

From that meeting things changed dramatically. The very next day, after the usual nightmare start, I received a phone call from student support to say that the inclusion officer I had met the day before, had been in to visit school. It had been decided that I should meet Dan daily for forty minutes in the student support centre, giving him a break in the day and contact with the one person he was so desperate to see. I remember the phone call well as I celebrated the fact that at last things could be different. Staff at the student support centre were quick to add that they had great reservations about the idea. I could see where they were coming from: all they ever saw was the nightmare that emerged when I left him in the mornings and that may be this new arrangement would just prolong the agony for Dan. One thing I did know was that what we had been trying was not working so this was at least something new. Also, deep down I did have a feeling that this could work.

The change began

The first day I went to visit Dan saw an almighty change in his behaviour. We had a relatively peaceful night and a morning that was not as traumatic as usual. When I arrived at student support they greeted me with a smile on their faces. Dan was sitting there eating one of the snacks I had left for him (as he could never face breakfast) and he too was smiling. We sat and hugged each other and he seemed happy for the first time in ages. Another immediate change that occurred after my daily visits started was the weekends; we got them back!

Since starting secondary school our weekends had been consumed by tears and irrational behaviour - they were something that we had learnt to dread! Not any longer; thank goodness we now had some respite amongst the total madness.

So it continued. Dan and I would plan our weekly timetable, carefully working out the best time for me to go in and meet him in the student support centre. We tried to change the time of my daily visit so Dan wouldn't get reliant on a certain time. We were also very mindful of not missing too many lessons of the same subject: (Dan had missed enough of his year 7 work already). In the beginning I visited Dan daily, meeting in the student support centre. We were always given a room to ourselves and in the beginning Dan would just hug me, sometimes just sit and cry. As time passed we used the time to talk, to write some of this, to do homework or just recap over the successes of the previous day. Slowly we reduced the number of days that I visited Dan at school, and by slowly, I really do mean slowly: by our tenth week Dan was doing two days on his own with varying success. I was determined to move slowly with this. If we moved too fast then all I would be doing was to confirm that school was ok **only** if I visited. By moving slowly hopefully Dan would learn to enjoy school life again and eventually not feel the need for my support, allowing me to withdraw completely. Again the staff at school agreed with this, they never rushed me or made me feel silly, we worked continuously as a team.

The Start of Cognitive Behaviour Therapy (CBT)

With further phone calls and determination Dan embarked on his course of cognitive behavioural therapy. My initial contact with the CBT therapist was on the telephone. I soon realised that she was going to make a real difference to our journey as she listened to everything I had to say, every minute detail of the traumatic past few weeks. For the first time in ages someone outside the family and the school seemed to really understand what we were going through. By the time we had finished on the phone (50 minutes later), I felt elated, hopeful and excited. The strange thing was that she seemed to think we were doing lots of things right already, I'd never really contemplated that we were doing things well - my reading, natural instincts and possibly teacher background had obviously helped!

The first appointment was just with me. I filled her in on all that was happening and again she told me how well we were doing, I actually started to believe it! She also explained that a lot of the CBT would be to work with myself and my husband; helping us to be Dan's therapist, supporting him daily. Dan was also excited about his first appointment which came the following week. They talked about his feelings, his worries and concerns and about how brave he was as he was confronting them daily, minute by minute. She likened him to a person who had a fear of heights pursuing his quest to react the summit of Mount Everest. By the end of the session Dan had really opened up. He amazed me how able he was at expressing his feelings to the therapist who was, really, a complete stranger.

Through CBT we learnt how to reduce Dan's anxiety by thinking of what it was that was worrying him. We would then gather evidence to reassure him that his worries were not in fact supported by facts and then finally we would reassess his worries hopefully seeing that they had diminished! Basically we needed to challenge Dan's thinking as he was allowing his thoughts to run away with him, he had lost the ability to think rationally: he was faced with a worry and then would blow things out of proportion - catastrophic thinking! To enable us to do this successfully we used carefully worded sheets to help guide us through this process, a process that with practise Dan would learn to do for himself once again - a process you and I do naturally without thinking. We learnt how to fill these sheets in. (Dan and I called them worry sheets!). Challenging his worries was hard for Dan to do, he found certain thoughts very painful and distressing. During one particular CAMHs session, which Dad took Dan to, Dan was asked to challenge what he was thinking when he felt he couldn't walk to school without me watching him walk to the top of the road, something that caused many problems in itself. Dan was obsessed with me standing on the street watching him and couldn't even contemplate reducing the distance over which I watched him, let alone letting me stop completely.   This session was hard for Dan, his Dad and indeed the CBT therapist!   That said I remember actually feeling thrilled that Dan had been   distressed and irrational throughout the session, thrilled because the CBT therapist could see the true terror that we were working with daily. A miracle however followed this appointment: Dan allowed me to write a timetable for the following month that saw this strange dependent routine diminish to simply saying goodbye to each other over the threshold of the door. It proved to us both that we could tackle his very worst fears - CBT was working! That said, we deserved this result as we had put in the effort; constantly filling in sheets and challenging Dan's every worry. I can't say it was easy. Sometimes Dan's face said it all when I grabbed yet another sheet from the side board, his face alone could have put me off, but it was so worth it!

Living on a Knife Edge

It would be so easy to sit and write every bad event that went on during the first few weeks of Dan's troubles but that would become repetitive and soul destroying. To summarise you could say Dan was living on a 'knife edge' – this is perhaps the best explanation of what was going on in his life. There were days when just one thing would set off a chain reaction of events leading to what felt like a total disaster!

To give a couple of examples:

One particular day Dan set off with his friend up the road. I stood outside the house watching him (our daily ritual) as he walked along, as usual throwing up. He had become quite a sight on our road as many neighbours were very familiar with our daily challenge of getting to school, tears, upset, running back to the house and more. Unfortunately this particular day was a foggy one so when Dan got to the top of the road he could not see me clearly to wave. Screaming and crying as he ran, he abandoned his friend and torpedoed back into my arms - how could he say good bye from the end of the street if he could not see me? We went back into the house where Dan continued to carry on and by now Tom was upset as well! That morning went from bad to worse; I had to take him in to student support where they tried to calm him as I left. He ended up spending the whole morning in there trying to convince the staff that he was really ill, how he desperately needed me and how no one understood him. Dan finally pulled himself together for the last lesson. All because of some fog!

Another day Dan set off as the bottle bank at Morrison's was being emptied. Just as he approached the top of the road he heard the unusual noise as the bottles fell into the truck, again he screamed his way back home convinced there was a bomb exploding!

Going out for me in the evenings was almost impossible for the first couple of months - housebound was a good definition of my situation. Many friends just said I had to go out, but the chaos this would cause really wasn't worth it. Knowing I couldn't be a complete hermit I started with short trips out: to the shops for a walk. In the beginning I would arrive home from these expeditions to be greeted by a tearful, terrified Dan sitting outside the house on the doorstep. It would then take hours for him to recover as he followed me around the house not daring to let me out of his sight. It was awful for me but also for his Dad who couldn't understand why his son didn't want to be left with him. This I found so hard as the joy of getting out was lost in the commotion it caused.

Another very hard week for us was the week the weather took a turn for the worse. Never did I think snow could cause such a problem. The snow was so bad that many local schools were closing. The anguish that this created for Dan as he prayed and bargained for his school to shut was immense. It became another obsession: logging on to the internet first thing in the morning, as well as having the radio on, desperately trying to find out the situation for the day ahead. His school did not shut at all over this period but by the end of it I too was praying for its closure, just to stop all the worries and traumas that the suspense was causing. On one of the days Tom's school shut and this was really hard for Dan to accept, another day where the house was full of upset and tears and another day when I had to get Dan into school by physically taking him in.

Frustrations

One of the hardest things for us to accept was that for every two steps forward we took, we seemed to take one and sometimes two or more steps back! This was obviously hardest for Dan as it was he who had to live through each and every experience. The family found it so hard as well for many reasons. Watching your son struggle in front of your eyes daily really hurt; all we wanted was to have our happy Dan back. I also found it particularly hard as it was me that was off work supporting Dan. With every traumatic day, I could see the date for my return to work slipping further and further away. Stopping work was necessary, in fact unavoidable really, but it meant that I had lost part of my identity at the same time and the guilt of not being in my class teaching, ate away at me daily. I had lost my distraction too. Whilst my husband carried on working he was able to lose himself in his work where as I would dwell on things all day long. Every time we solved a problem another one would emerge and the joy of the success was very quickly wiped away. It felt like we were literally trying to plug a hole in a sinking ship: when one hole was plugged, a new one would open and we would frantically try to find some method of filling it before we sunk. Through trial and error, the advice of student support, the cognitive behavioural therapist and the educational psychologist we learnt how to tackle Dan's problems by supporting him to find his own solutions.

A break through

Having come up with a theory that this nightmare had come about due to Dan's fragile emotional state due to his multiple tic disorder; the awareness he had of his own mortality; and the stress of the transition process; something happened to confirm our theory even further...

There was always a slight doubt in everybody's minds that Dan could actually have some kind of physical complaint that was causing him to be so ill. As we got to know his symptoms more and more and as we learnt what triggered them, the idea of a physical illness was becoming less and less supported. It was however decided that the doctors would not be doing their job if they did not send Dan to the hospital for a health check. This appointment eventually came through (a 3 month wait) but it was so worth having. During the appointment, with a remarkable doctor, Dan was asked numerous questions about his symptoms and he was also examined thoroughly. The worry about his tablets also came up and the doctor dealt with this information so well. Her immediate response was to get her calculator out and to illustrate to Dan just how low the dose he was on was; she then compared this to what he could actually be put on safely. These concrete facts along with her wonderful bedside manner really impressed Dan and it was like a magic light switch, suddenly he seemed to have made 'friends' with his medicine.

On the way home Dan and I spoke about the appointment and I asked him how he felt about his tablets now. He seemed happy at last, at peace with it all, this proved to be a massive turning point for us! Now that we had managed to remove this enormous concern it felt like we actually had a chance of solving the rest of his worries and anxieties!

Logging our success

As progress was so slow it seemed that things were going on for ever, it was hard to see the steps forward that we were making as these would get muddled in the disasters of the day. It became important to us to log our progress, to reflect on them regularly. We found many methods of doing this including the following.

Diary

To help us monitor and recognise our success Dan and I began to write a weekly diary. In this we wrote how we felt the week had gone. We split the recording into 3 areas: progress and success; issues and concerns; overall feelings.

In itself the diary was very therapeutic; writing down our feelings enabled us to get out in the open what we were thinking - it opened the doors for us to talk. It allowed us to look back and see clearly the success and progress we were making – very useful during the times where we all felt flat and fed up.

Daily records

At the end of every day we initially found ourselves going over and over the day, dissecting every part of it. We soon came to realise that we needed to limit the dissection of the day to a five to ten minute period. We also needed to stop dwelling on the negatives and start celebrating the positives. We therefore drew up a chart and each evening we would write down four positives about the day. Sometimes these were easy to find such as: I've completed the whole day today on my own, I've joined table tennis club. Sometimes they were harder to find: I walked home today, I didn't cry this morning; I got very upset and recovered quickly. Again the chart was great for reminding ourselves of how far we had come.

Other useful tips

Part of the point of writing this for me is so that other people might gain some comfort from it. That they might realise that they are not the only ones going through this all consuming trouble. Through trial and error Dan and I came up with many solutions to problems some obvious, some not so. By explaining all of these hopefully it will be helpful to others.

Praise, praise and more praise

In a time where you really are at loss with what to say and do, when your son is acting in a way that is totally alien to his usual nature, it would be so easy to lose your cool. There were many times when we could have just lost control and shouted at Dan (we were guilty of that on a couple of occasions - we are all only human!). We soon learnt however that Dan did not mean anything he said or did, he was not responsible for his actions when he was out of control crying and distressed. He didn't mean to be unkind with his words, he didn't mean to cry all evening bringing the mood in the house to an all time low and he certainly didn't mean to feel so awful and desperate. We therefore had no right to be cross with him. We tried hard to be patient and loving and to praise every time he did something that was hard for him. This could have been as simple as saying 'well done you got dressed yourself' or 'I'm impressed that you went to one lesson today Dan - amazing.' It wasn't hard to praise Dan as he was so intent on settling in. He was determined to be like everyone else who did not have their Mum visit them daily. Dan was incredible to work with and most definitely the bravest person that I know! (As stated by the CBT therapist as well).

Rewards

As Dan achieved the goals that he had set for himself we thought of rewards. These were not financial monsters, more rewards involving time spent together. We would watch home movies; have a special dinner (Chinese being Dan's favourite), play games; have an extra late night; have family days out. They were always special times and the whole family looked forward to them knowing that they celebrated success.

Support your child, don't take over (hard to do!)

In the beginning we were so shocked by Dan's behaviour that we almost wrapped him up in cotton wool. We constantly reassured him that things would be ok and ended up trying to solve problems for him. At the time this was the easiest option for everyone involved and calmed Dan down the fastest. Quickly as time progressed we realised that we were actually de-skilling Dan: we were making him even more reliant on us. We had forgotten the very basics of parenting, help your child to help themselves. Turn around questions that they ask you by asking them questions in return, make them think of their own solutions. It wasn't easy to do as Dan was so distressed we just wanted to take away the pain for him, but we did it. We knew that in the end this would give him the ability to solve his own problems with support, just as he had done before all this began.

Don't avoid the problem

It would have been so easy to allow Dan to avoid all the things that he found so hard. I could have easily kept him at home on the days he simply refused to go into school on his own, I never wanted to drive him down and force him through the doors, it would have been much easier to sit at home cuddling him. Equally it would have been easy to pick him up from school every day never insisting that he made his own way home. When we sat down and wrote the timetable for the following week's visits it would have been easy to miss the same subjects, the ones Dan felt uncomfortable with, for whatever reason, but we didn't. We always faced our problems head on; avoiding them was never an option! Had we allowed ourselves to do this then we would never have made any progress at all, it wasn't easy though!

Listen to your Instincts

In the beginning we were constantly looking for advice, opinions and ideas from others. We did have our own ideas about what was happening to Dan, but kept thinking that others must know more. However, as time passed it became apparent that in fact no one else knew much more than us. More than that in fact: as Dan's parents, we needed to take charge, trust our instincts and believe in ourselves. On a few occasions when were unsure of what to do, if we just relaxed and trusted our instincts then often the best decision was made.

Fight for your Child - Never Rest!

It became very clear early on that if I'd left everything to run to its natural NHS course, i.e. waiting times and services available, then we would still be waiting for certain appointments now! I chased every appointment offered, I visited the doctors weekly and expressed our distress and upset constantly, I never let any promises made by the professional's drop: I was determined to get Dan all the help he deserved and I really feel that this attitude made all the difference, even if we did annoy a lot of people along the way! I must say that the support from our doctors was fantastic too, support for Dan and definitely support for me. Often they were as frustrated as me at the time it took to get things moving: I will always be grateful for their time and help, thank you seems hardly enough.

Bargaining tools

As new suggestions were made to help Dan I would seize every bargaining tool I could to use with him. On the day that I was given the go ahead to visit Dan daily I decided to use such a bargaining tool. I told him that I would visit him as long as he walked himself to school in the mornings. No longer could he allow himself to get into such a state that I would have to take him into student support myself. Like a miracle Dan fulfilled his part of the bargain and on the whole this was the end of my early morning trips to school. Bargaining with Dan allowed us to make big jumps in our progress and made him feel that he was in charge and in control as well. He liked the idea that if I did something for him then he would need to reciprocate the favour. He certainly knew that I had made a huge commitment to him by taking time off work on sick (stress). Taking time off was a fabulous bargaining tool in itself as Dan realised that he had to make an equal commitment to the process as well, after all it was his journey.

Find someone in the same situation

One of the biggest breakthroughs for us was finding another family in the same position. This encounter happened early on in our journey. It happened to be someone Dan and I already knew from primary school. I can clearly remember the day we found out that this other year 7 child was also struggling to settle into secondary school, I felt excited and almost elated to have found someone in the same boat (felt a bit guilty about that)! What resulted was a close friendship between another mother and me. Dan and her son even met up a few times and we would all discuss as many of the positive advances we were making as well as sharing concerns and worries. We'd send each other texts and make phone calls of support. This was great as no matter how hard other people tried to understand our situation it was almost impossible to do. Knowing someone else was in the same boat and was talking from a real understanding of the situation was so comforting and made us feel less alone.

Getting to know everyone who is in contact with your child

Half the problem of Dan being in secondary school was knowing who Dan was talking about when he was particularly worried about a teacher or indeed when he found a certain teacher helpful. Student support helped considerably here as they would send reminders out to all the staff in the registers if Dan was struggling with something. They would also go and see a particular teacher if Dan was especially worried about a certain subject or simply falling behind - all of this was invaluable. One thing we found that helped considerably however was actually meeting these members of staff in person. The PE teacher for example seemed to have something special about him that Dan connected with, this we found highly amusing as PE had never been one of Dan's favourite subjects to say the least. One particular day I bumped into the PE teacher and was able to thank him for his commitment to Dan, this we feel helped to cement Dan's relationship further. We made a point of meeting his lovely form tutor, his head of year and indeed the head teacher, all of which allowed us to communicate more intimately with Dan about his school relationships, which all helped to make him feel that we were there supporting him. Obviously our relationship with student support was clear for Dan to see and the fact that we were all working as a team (Dan being a major part of that team) definitely was a help for everyone involved.

Make rules to help establish desired behaviour

Throughout this journey Dan's behaviour was quite irrational and traumatic. He would lose control of what he was saying and doing. For a very sensitive and intelligent young man he would say and do things that were not typical. To help us gain control of some of his action we introduced rules. An example of this was when he started to ring and text me from school. These phone calls / texts got us nowhere and just served to upset Dan and I further. We therefore introduced the rule that he could not phone or text during the day once he had stepped inside the schools gates. He could ring on the way to and from school if he thought it was really necessary, but that was it. We wrote these rules down in our diary and referred to them regularly. Dan was great as he realised that these were boundaries he had to keep to and it certainly helped me when things got turbulent and confusing.

Occasionally there were times when you had to bend a rule slightly. An example of this was after the Christmas holidays (returning to school after a holiday was always hard). Dan was down to three days of visits from me and the rule was we had to keep it at this. To help him to settle back in we bent my visiting rule for the first week. Instead of not visiting him at all on his first solo day of the week I met him away from school for lunch - strictly speaking we had not broken the rules as I had not gone into school!

Don't go backwards

No matter how slowly we travelled forward on this incredible journey, and boy did it feel **so slow** at times, we made sure that we never allowed ourselves to go backwards: if we introduced a new rule to follow (that we all agreed to) then we could not withdraw it. An example of this would be when we reduced the number of days I would visit Dan at school. When we first reduced my visits from five to four, Dan found the day I did not visit so immensely traumatic he would spend most of it in student support. No matter how hard it was for him (and me) he knew he had to get used to it as this was a decision we could not go back on. The same went for when we cut down the distance I would watch Dan walk down the street in the morning, once we had cut ten meters off the distance there was no going back. This was an invaluable but tough rule to follow

Remember you can recover

Just when we thought that we had 'nailed' a problem, that we were making good progress, something would happen that meant that Dan would take a step (or two!) backwards. In the beginning these setbacks would not only shake Dan's world but they would also shake ours as well. This was where student support would come in to their own as they would convince us that we could recover, the setbacks didn't mean that we were back to square one. They actually likened the setbacks to a person following a weight watchers plan: it was possible to blow your diet one day and then pick it up again the next. Initially this was hard to believe, but eventually with support and help we learned to realise that this was indeed true, so much so that Dan started to realise this as well. As time passed we were actually able to use the setbacks as experiences to learn from - it was amazing!

Maintaining friendships

Something that definitely helped Dan along the way was to make sure that his friendships were maintained. No matter how exhausted and tired we all were Dan and Tom would have friends over at least twice a week and even at weekends. This was so important as all Dan's friends saw at school was an upset crying wreck, they could not see the real Dan anymore - even we couldn't. In the beginning this was so hard because at his worst Dan seemed unable to play / interact with the friends we would invite over. All he wanted to do was to sit and hug me; he would seek me out leaving his friend in another room. I found myself sending him back to his friend or alternatively spending a lot of my time playing with them both, filling in the gaps of conversation, trying to be the life and soul of the party. This paid off in the end as Dan became more and more confident and happy to play. It also helped as he refused to go to anyone else's for tea; he didn't want to extend his day away from me any further. If we hadn't invited these friends back to our house then I think he would have lost many of them. As it happened his friendships were not a casualty of what was happening to him and this was important for his continued recovery.

Don't forget the rest of the family

As hard as it is when you are totally and utterly consumed with one of your children you must not forget the other. Tom was really struggling with all of this in the first few weeks as we were solely concentrating (understandably) on Dan. It soon became apparent that we could not afford to do this as Tom was suffering too. As soon as we realised this we started to concentrate more on Tom, making sure that while one of us dealt with Dan the other was free to be with Tom. We would engineer weekends where we took it in turns to take Tom out of the mad house and keep him busy and happy with other activities. We also tried to make time for us to be together as a couple and to distract ourselves as we worried about what the next day would bring. Me time was not as easy to find due to the nature of the problem, but it improved as we progressed along our journey.

Much of this is written in the first person but I need to make it clear at this part that Dan's Dad played a very active part in this journey. He was there at all the decisions, on the phone to help whenever he could and certainly there to praise and love and care for Dan. It is only because we jointly decided that I should take the time off work, whilst he carried on working, that I implemented and saw through most of our decisions; it was really hard for both of us for different reasons.

Useful sayings (mantra)

Dan and I spent so much time talking together that we would come up with helpful sayings to get us through the difficult times. These included sayings such as: "this time will pass"; "keep calm, think, solve"; and "what would you tell a friend?" amongst others. "What would you tell a friend?" was a fabulous one as it allowed Dan to more calmly arrive at a solution to a problem. He would simply think of the problem and then imagine a friend of his having that problem, considering what he would advise them to do. For some reason this would help Dan as he seemed to think more clearly about the solution without getting so personally involved. As well as this, his advice to others was always so much kinder than his advice to himself! We wrote all these sayings down on pieces of card, laminated them and then fitted them together on a key ring. Dan would keep this key ring in his school bag and get it out and read the sayings when he needed to.

Don't feel guilty and don't be hard on yourself

There have been so many times in all of this where I have felt guilty. I have gone over and over in my head as to whether I have done the right thing. At times I have lost the plot, I have shouted and cried in front of Dan, said things I wish I hadn't. Strangely these times have often been great turning points in our journey despite my feelings of guilt. To be honest it probably did Dan good to see the impact his problems had on the rest of us. Guilt gets us nowhere, what's done is done.

Work was a problem for me as it was constantly on my mind, adding if anything to my stress. If I had to replay this time again (god forbid) I would have tried harder to put work out of my mind. The guilt I have felt for not being in class, not teaching, letting people down has been debilitating at times, a waste. I have done what I had to do, surely what any mother would do in my situation; I don't regret a minute of it; I am proud to hear myself say that.

Finally – be strong

Through all of this I have felt that I have had to be the strongest person I could possibly be; I have had to summon every piece of strength in me to see this through. There have been many times where I would have liked to crawl away under a rock; to throw in the towel; to give up, but that would have got us nowhere. There have been challenges that have seemed too big for me so how they must have felt for Dan I can only imagine. The hardest one for me was trying to break the routine of watching Dan walk up the street. Dan felt he had to have me in sight on this short journey and by the time we got to the fourth week of watching him I almost felt as if I had to be there too, that maybe, just maybe he was right - maybe he would crumble if I wasn't there. He had managed to convince me that he needed me to be there in case he was sick, in case he had forgotten something, in case he fell out with his friend! I knew that this was an obsession that had to stop to restore Dan's independence but it was so hard for us both to face.

Dan could always come up with a reason why I had to be there and I just kept thinking that if it helped...then maybe I should watch him, it was the least I could do. Really all I was doing was to confirm his anxious thoughts - I wasn't helping at all! I admitted this to the CBT therapist, I admitted that I too was scared and it was then that I made myself begin the process of supporting Dan to stop this obsession.

It was then that we drew up a timetable together, slowly reducing the distance on the road that I would watch him. Before, when we had discussed this, I had not been strong enough to see it through. Dan had seen my insecurities and picked up on them making it so hard for him to believe that he could do this. This time I was adamant, I showed him I had true belief in his ability to succeed even though I had such doubts myself. This took so much strength I can't begin to tell you, but from the minute we sat down to solve the problem it took one month to the day to succeed. Dan can now walk out of the house and take himself to school like any other eleven year old without his Mum watching him as he goes...SUCCESS!

Where are we up to now?

Our journey is by no means over. We are now nearly half way through the academic year and I have been off work for fifteen weeks. My sick note carries on for another five weeks when I really hope that I can return to work (and my life) knowing that we have things here under control. It won't be the end of it all by any means. By the time I return to work Dan will be coping with three days at school on his own, I will still visit him on the others. He will be walking to and from school confidently with his friends and I will not have to watch him down the street or be there for him the second he gets home. We will continue to move forward in our progress until Dan realises that he can do it on his own, when he no longer feels the need for my presence (he already asks me to leave student support before me so no one knows that I'm his Mum!). No doubt he will have bad days when he takes himself to the friendly faces in the student support centre, where he has to rely heavily on all the skills and tools that he has learnt over the course of these months. In a way he is lucky as he has learnt so much from this experience, invaluable lessons! We too have learnt lots as a family, we have been through the mill but we are now closer than ever. We realise what wonderful and supportive friends we have; they have kept us sane at times with their texts and phone calls. (Thank you so much, you know who you are!). We have marvelled at the generosity of strangers who do so much more than their job descriptions state. We have had our faith restored in the children of today as Dan's friends have been just incredible through all of this. In a way it's been a fantastic journey!

Dan has come so far it's incredible, we can now put this down as a blip in his life - **we feel sure of our happy ending whilst acknowledging that there will be more blips along the way. (Did I actually say that?).**

This is how I have seen the last few months in our house but this wouldn't be a full story if the other members of the family didn't say their bit. I therefore pass you over to Dan himself followed by young Tom who has been a star through all of this and not forgetting his Dad. Dan may be the bravest person I have ever known but Tom certainly wins the medal for

kindness and patience and best little brother award...

P.S.

A few more weeks have passed since I last wrote in this book and more positive things have been happening....

Dan has received an outstanding half year report which brought tears to all of our eyes; he has managed a sleep over at a friend's (very successfully); Mum and Dad have been out one evening whilst Dan and Tom were left with a sitter - all further evidence that life is on the mend yippee!!!

What Happened To Me? By Dan

I was so looking forward to starting Secondary School with the thought of all that freedom. Being able to chuck snow balls on the way to school, pushing my mates into puddles, chucking leaves at friends: all that freedom!

After my day visit up to the school I was left feeling a bit nervous and the thought that I would like to stay at primary school was there. I told myself this is where I have to be, this is what I'm going to do so I'd better start looking forward to it: so I did - up until the first few days of starting School that is. I soon realised that I would do anything to avoid being at School because all I wanted was my Mum. I was so scared of the teachers, scared of the older children, red marks, detentions, not getting my tie done up correctly. In fact I was pretty scared of everything! This fear made me do all sorts of things. I lied to stay at home or to be sent home and some of my lies worked. One day I made up how ill I was (although I did feel ill); I begged my Mum to let me stay at home and she did. This helped as I could rest and it made me want to do it more and more. There were lots of times I did feel awful and I realise now that because I lied no one believes me when I really do feel ill.

The first week

The first week at School was probably my best even though I cried all the time in the mornings and evenings at home. I never cried at school - I wouldn't let myself. I cried at home because I dreaded going to school. I was scared of everything I just wanted to be at home. To get me through the week I kept talking to myself, it's sad but I did, and I got through the first week.

The next few weeks

Lots happened in the next few weeks. On the second Monday I felt ill and was sent to Matron who sent me home. I felt dizzy and sick, generally awful. Mum had to leave work to come and collect me, she sat down and talked to Matron, she cried. I felt so bad as I knew I was putting Mum through so much but I couldn't help it. We went home and everything got sorted. I felt so much better at home; Dad came home from work to look after me as Mum had to go back to work. Grandma came up the next day from Cambridge and I stayed off another day. I felt so much safer and happier at home but I also wanted to go back to School to see how I felt there.

So much happened in the next few weeks it's hard to remember everything but here are a few things...

I tried so hard to settle but I couldn't, I felt so unhappy it was horrible. One day I got so upset and felt so bad that I actually fainted in student support, it was scary. Mum took me to the doctors who said that my body had shut down but it was ok now, so I went back to school.

Another time I really remember feeling awful is the time I was asked to sort out my tie in French. As I walked into our French class Miss told me and a few others to go back outside. She told us to sort our ties out. When I had sorted mine she again told me it wasn't right. This made me hate and dread French lessons. We eventually told student support and they took me to see the French teacher. I couldn't believe it as she apologised to me and said it was just what she did; ties were her thing!

Mornings were awful. I threw up all the time on the way to school. As I walked with my friend he got annoyed and eventually ran off as he hates the sound and sight of sick. This made me run home and Mum would give me a lift. Often she would take me to student support and the goodbye we had was horrible. Student support had to pull me off Mum, why couldn't she have stayed until I had calmed down? Sometimes I could not recover from this and I would spend the whole day in student support. If they had let Mum stay until I had calmed down then I would have been fine and I would have been able to go to lessons.

Why wouldn't the Doctors do anything to help me?

Mum took me to the doctors lots of times in the first few weeks. The doctors weren't really helping me at all; they just made judgements about me. They never actually checked me; it felt like everything they said they were making up as they always said I wasn't poorly so that I would go away. They said that it was anxiety and I HATED that word (I still do). I wanted to shout at anyone who mentioned it: "I WAS POORLY!" Anxiety is a tiny thing you get when you have a test, they were basically saying all my being sick and ill was down to a tiny feeling of anxiety - it wasn't! I still wanted to go to the doctors each time. I wanted to keep going until they said I was ill, I had a bug or something. Then I could go "HA" in everyone's face. Also if I had a bug then they could cure it and it would go away.

Eventually I knew what was wrong: MY TABLETS

In my sessions after school with Miss I had learnt to

use a worry scale. It let you rate how worried you were about something on a scale from 0-10. One night when Mum was talking to me she asked me if I thought my problems were due to me being worried about my tablets. When she asked me I started to cry as I thought about it, I realised I had a 10 on my worry scale for my tablets. The side effects were so dangerous that I was really scared that I COULD DIE! How would you feel if you knew your tablets were dangerous and when the symptoms that you were told to look out for happened, nobody listened to you? What was even worse was **I couldn't** tell if my symptoms were happening because of anxiety or the side effects of the tablets, I was so confused. If it was my side effects then I needed my Mum to see me just in case anything happened. I had to have her but nobody would listen. After we realised what the problem was lots of doctors told me my tablets were fine but I couldn't believe them. What could I do? I needed to take my tablets as I hated my tics so much - it was so hard.

The Student Support Centre

The people there were really nice and helped me through some struggling times. It was a relief to know that if I couldn't cope with my lessons that I had somewhere to go. (It would have been horrible to just sit in lessons throwing up and crying in front of everyone). They even made me hot water bottles when I had belly aches and cool packs when I felt hot. They did annoy me though, even though I knew that they were always trying to help me. They annoyed because they didn't always believe how ill I felt. I was so scared that it could be the tablets making me ill and that by not believing me, something terrible could happen to me. Every time I went there upset, they always talked about anxiety and emotions and deep breathing. I found this very hard to talk about and I still do! Sometimes I would just sit and cry and shout but I always knew that they cared. It was great when they agreed to let Mum come in each day, this made a massive difference and I felt as if I could manage. If I could see Mum then she could check I was fine. They also gave me extra lessons after school to help me cope; I did these with another boy who found school hard – it was good.

I know that they helped Mum a lot by talking to her on the phone and when she came in; that helped me too.

Cognitive Behaviour Therapy

At last people were beginning to listen to me and they said I needed cognitive behaviour therapy, I couldn't wait for it. I couldn't wait partly because I would be able to miss school and if it really was anxiety then I could get some help. I felt like it was ages until my first appointment, why did it have to be so long; this made feel so upset and angry and of course sick.

The first appointment was ok for me but I was nervous. The lady asked me questions and listened to me. It felt really good that someone was finally listening to me. (I have always found it so strange how they talk to you, it seems so weird, it's too hard to explain how they talk). She said I was doing very well and that I was brave as well. I got really upset on the first occasion because I had to say things that were difficult for me. I remember crying all the way home and still Mum said I had to go back to school.

In the second session we talked some more and I felt sometimes that I had to say what people wanted me to say rather than what I wanted to say. We kept filling in worry sheets to try and reduce my worries but this didn't always work. I could do it in my head but it wasn't so easy on paper. I felt that I was being pushed to reduce my worry rating when I didn't want to. Although this is how I felt, I knew she was pushing me for a reason and it did work. We did a worry sheet to help me get to school in the morning without Mum watching me. This was so horrible. I didn't want Mum to stop watching me, I needed her. These sessions were the hardest thing I have ever done in my life but I am glad I did it. Now that I can walk to school without Mum watching me it is brilliant and I know that the sheets helped me do this. The lady really helped Mum as well and she said to me often that she needed the help too.

The Christmas Holidays

I felt fine over the Christmas holidays. I went to see

a pantomime, I spent time with my family and I opened loads of presents. I built Lego models and had a lovely Christmas dinner. Everything felt normal! I didn't feel as if I needed Mum all the time because I didn't feel poorly. The weekend before school started I had a bit of a wobble on the Friday night but then we had a busy weekend with the cinema and friends which was good. The Sunday night was not good. I felt weird and started crying about school. Mum and I filled in one of the cognitive behavioural sheets to try to help; Mum's talking helped more than the sheet!

My tablets are fine!!!!

Because I was always feeling so ill Mum and I were sent to the hospital to see a doctor who was going to check I was alright. She examined me and said I was fine. She also talked to me lots which was nice. She told me that it was really unlikely that I felt awful because of my tablets. She said I was only on a quarter of what a child could be on let alone an adult. I really believed her as she took a lot of time to explain it all to me. All the other doctors had missed out telling me about my dosage being so small. If they had told me this then I would have believed them too. I felt BRILLIANT! I was so relieved that none of this was due to my tablets but at the same time I felt sad as it could take ages to cure my anxiety.

How do I feel now?

I am now going to school 3 days a week on my own. When I wake up I sometimes feel glum but I know I have to go. I don't feel as poorly as I used to although some days I do feel awful.

Secondary school is fine, my friends are great. Some lessons are boring but others are fun like: PE, Science, Art, Music, Technology and there are other ones too. If you are someone like me and you are going through a tough time I would say read this book, it might help. Don't give up, keep going. It is the hardest thing to do but I'm doing it.

I really do think I will get settled at school and that I won't feel poorly all the time and I will be fine **without** Mum.

My Big Brother. By Tom

Dan has not been very well. He has been sick and he has been scared and he has been crying a lot. It felt like he cried all the time. All he has wanted has been Mum. It has been annoying in the mornings because all Dan wanted was Mum. When he has left for school I have been looking forward to spending time with her but he has often rung and we have had to go out and help him. So then I haven't been able to have any time with her. This has made me feel sad and upset as I have had to wait six and a half hours for school to finish before I can see Mum again! When the day has finished I have at last had some time with Mum. This has been getting a lot lot better as Dan has been settling in better and so has been happier and more fun.

I want him to settle in completely and be like he was when he was in primary school. Mum and Dad have tried to make some time for me. It has been very hard for the whole family but it is getting better.

My perspective! By Dad

So what is my view on this?

Mum, Dan and Tom have already said so much in their parts and I am not totally convinced that I can add any more that will be of any use to anyone. But it is only right that I share my experiences, not only for the benefit of any other dads out there but for me also. So here goes...

I guess as a father, a connection to your own children is not necessarily as strong as that between mother and child. However, Dan and I have actually always had a very close relationship; I don't know if that is an oldest child and father thing, but it was certainly always there. And it still is I realise when I take a step back and look closely. However, Dan's whole post-tic illness, his severe separation anxiety, did leave me feeling out on a limb on many occasions, I suppose because of his dependence on mum. It is crucial for me to realise that this was actually part of his illness though and nothing personal. But, well I guess I need to take a real step back to the time of his tics.

I remember back to the days when the raising of an eyebrow from time to time seemed totally innocuous, a nervous reaction or just a child's strange habit whilst relaxing at the end of a busy day. These were the days of his year 6 SATS tests after all. It wasn't really until a number of his tics, that had each steadily developed, started combining and poor old Dan sat in evenings with face and neck contorting beyond comprehension, that mum and I realised something more was amiss. I don't need to go into much more detail because that has been covered elsewhere; my purpose is to convey how I was feeling.

At this stage Dan was not unwell as such, there was nothing to be overly concerned about; after all his health did not appear to be at risk. But was it? My immediate response would be that we, (I), should have done something earlier, but recollecting those days, I realise that we, (mum), had in fact been taking Dan to the Doctors regularly. Of course, most of those appointments took place during the working day, an inconvenient time for a working dad, and perhaps that is where I feel the gap began to grow, or rather the dependence on his mum grew.

As we sought and secured medical assistance, the dependence on mum grew even further, I believe, because it was mum that went to the majority of appointments with Dan. It also seemed logical for mum and Dan to repeatedly attend such sessions together as mum held all the knowledge of the previous sessions and could convey information more easily. Mum has always liked verbatim reports about such meetings anyway, so it seemed natural for her to attend than for me to "report back" every detail! (This makes me chuckle slightly as this also applies to phone calls, meetings with friends etc etc and mum has in fact admitted to me that she prefers to attend the appointments herself anyway!)

Mum often told me of Dan's concerns as he did not seem willing to discuss them with me. Although to this day I am not sure why, I can say this is no longer the case. Why? I think because once we finally got appointments early on with CAMHs, I was able to attend more of these appointments with Dan; probably accidental as the appointments themselves happened to correspond on a day that mum taught. So finally an element of dependence on a parent did shift back to me. And whilst the actual appointments themselves did not directly involve me (CAMHs prefer the child to attend the session with just their counsellor) they did allow the bond between father and son to rekindle.

It was then that I believe I realised it was fundamental to our father son bond that I attempt to involve myself more, however possible, to attend with Dan as often as possible. It allowed him to talk with me again about his concerns and not just his mum. So rather than by design and more by necessity I believe we stumbled across a solution. My advice to any other dads in the same situation would be that they absolutely must get involved, no matter what the consequence at work. In fact, I remember one particular morning after an appointment with Dan (I think) that I was finding everything too much to cope with and decided to stop off before going in to work; a chance to reflect mostly (partly to have a quiet cry). On arriving at work, I decided to tell my management what was going on in my life. It was surprisingly easy as it happens and my manager was exceptionally understanding. This proves that it does pay to talk and be honest. From that day, on the understanding of course that I do my best to make up time out of the office, management was totally sympathetic for my need to take time off work to attend appointments with Dan.

I think that was a real turning point for me, realising that whilst everything seemed fine, mum was actually almost entirely sorting things out in the background and life almost seemed normal. Attending with Dan helped me realise this was not the case and helped me explore how I could support mum, Dan and of course Tom. Poor old Tom, so left out "in the cold". I just hope that he is young enough that he will be able to compartment away this awful time of his life and not carry it through adolescence with him. And of course, poor old Dan. This is an experience he is much less likely to forget and he will carry this through into his teens. Mum of course will not be able forget and I am sure so much of this will play on her mind for months, years to come.

And me, well this had been a journey for me too. One of self and of my family development. I have been able to look back and realise the utmost importance of being involved as a parent, as a dad, and not to sit back confident in the knowledge that someone else is dealing with the problem. It is so easy to not become involved and not necessarily deliberately, but I know of so many dads that would not dream of "demeaning" themselves in everyday affairs like this! I am just so glad that I was able to offer some support, however limited it might be.

Observations! By the cats

Meow meow meow....poor old Dan purrrrrrrrr!

www.ingramcontent.com/pod-product-compliance
Lightning Source LLC
Chambersburg PA
CBHW031140270326
41931CB00007B/636